keeping your

love

keeping your

love alive

love

love

love alive

keeping your

love

keeping your

Presented to:

Joe & Jen

From:

Paul & Sharon
May God bless
your marriage!

And now these three remain:
faith, hope and love.

But the greatest of these is *love.*

1 Corinthians 13:13

Keeping Your Love Alive
Copyright 1999 by The Zondervan Corporation
ISBN 0-310-97809-2

Requests for information should be addressed to:

ZondervanPublishingHouse
    Grand Rapids, Michigan 49530
    http://www.zondervan.com

Compiler: Doris Rikkers
Design: Big Cat Marketing Communications

Printed in China
00 01 02/HK/5 4 3 2 1

keeping your
love alive

love

keeping your

creative tips for lasting romance

Zondervan *Gifts*
We have a gift for inspiration™

*R*omance isn't reserved just for the young, and neither is it reserved for the bedroom. Being affectionate, thoughtful, and kind at other times will spill over into your love life. We all like to be nurtured and cherished. Phone calls, notes that say, "I love you," cooking your mate's favorite dish, giving a bouquet of flowers, holding hands, a peck on the cheek, a wink across the room, and saying loving and endearing things to each other will add romance to your relationship.

David and Claudia Arp

Love is the ultimate good. It lifts us outside ourselves. Love sees beyond the normal range of human vision—over walls of resentment and barriers of betrayal. Love rises above the petty demands and conflicts of life and inspires our spirit to transcend who we are tempted to settle for: decent, but merely mediocre. Love aims higher. Unencumbered by self-absorption, love charms us to reach our ideal. Love allures us with a hint of what might be possible.

Les and Leslie Parrott

*T*o form a forever relationship, you will need a Love-centered marriage. The love you have at the beginning with its intensely personal quality of belonging and possessing fluctuates because it is fed by feelings, and feelings change, especially if needs and desires are not being met. But the God of Love has made his own love available to each of us. That love, which the Bible calls agape, never changes. It is unconditional and does not depend on a person's behavior. It goes right on showing kindness to the beloved, no matter what, because it is controlled not by our emotions, but by our will. The ability to love this way is a gift from God through his Son Jesus Christ; his love channeled through us blesses our mate and our marriage.

Ed Wheat

Greet one another with a kiss of love.
1 Peter 5:14

*Houses and wealth are inherited from parents,
but a prudent wife is from the* LORD.
Proverbs 19:14

Love one another deeply, from the heart.
1 Peter 1:22

His banner over me is love.
Song of Songs 2:4

Enjoy life with your wife, whom you love.
Ecclesiastes 9:9

Tips for Loving Her

Write her a love poem for her birthday.
Give her a foot massage.
Tell her how attractive she is.
Pray for her.
Surprise her with breakfast in bed.
Hold her hand in public.
Learn to enjoy shopping.
Fix dinner for her.
Value what she says.
Tell her how proud you are of her.

*L*ove without intimacy is only a hormonal illusion. One cannot desire another person over the long haul without really knowing that person.

Intimacy has a "best friend" or "soul mate" quality about it. We all want someone who knows us better than anyone else—and still accepts us. And we want someone who holds nothing back from us, someone who trusts us with personal secrets. Intimacy fills our heart's deepest longings for closeness and acceptance.

People who have successfully built an intimate relationship know its power and comfort, but they also know that taking the emotional risks that allow intimacy to happen isn't easy. Without careful nurturing, intimacy withers.

Les and Leslie Parrott

*L*ife is a series of adjustments. Changes are as certain as the seasons. So embrace change. Greet it as a welcomed guest. If you don't like the way things are right now, don't panic—more changes may be just up the road! Grab the initiative and do what you can do to put more fun into your life and more life into your friendship with your spouse. You can start anytime and it can start with you!

David and Claudia Arp

*O*f all the little expressions of love—a box of chocolates, a handwritten poem, or a bouquet of handpicked wildflowers—I think my favorite is a good old-fashioned kiss on the lips. Whether it be the gratuitous kind that comes with greeting my husband after a day at work or his surprising ambush kiss while standing in line at the grocery, I always feel especially loved when Les gives me a simple kiss.

Les and Leslie Parrott

I'm a big believer in marriage. I have never seen happier, more deeply satisfied people than men and women who have made their marriages work. But neither have I met many people in highly successful marriages who got there without an enormous expenditure of energy and determination. There were times when they simply had to be "willful." Virtually every successful marriage requires all kinds of willpower. Sometimes issues arise and the partners don't have the necessary skills to manage them. They essentially have two choices: give up and run away, or get about the task of developing the required skills. Partners with willpower always adopt the second alternative. They wouldn't think of giving up. They are ready to go to work on the problem, ready to do whatever they must to keep their marriage healthy for a lifetime.

Dr. Neil Clark Warren

Ideas for Dating

Go out for coffee and reminisce about
a date you had that neither of you will forget.

Visit a museum.

Go shopping and buy a Christmas tree ornament for each other.

Stay home, eat popcorn, and watch your favorite video.

Plant flowers or a tree together.

Look through each other's childhood pictures. Pick out the favorite
one of your spouse and share why you chose that one.

Go bowling together.

Eat out at an Italian restaurant for dinner.

See a romantic movie together.

Take a day off to be together.

*i*f you want your marital relationship to deepen, it is very important that you learn to be flexible. I believe there is nothing as important to you or your family as a good, loving relationship with your husband. Your flexibility can make your husband feel really special and can keep that "spark" in your relationship. When he comes home and sees that you are willing to set aside your schedule for an unrushed conversation, he feels valued and loved. Your schedule is important, I realize. However, you need to maintain a balance by being able to set aside your priorities from time to time to pay special attention to your husband and his needs. That's genuine love.

Gary Smalley

Be completely humble and gentle;
be patient, bearing with one another in love.
Make every effort to keep the unity of
the Spirit through the bond of peace.
Ephesians 4:2–3

Love must be sincere.
Romans 12:9

He who covers over an offense promotes love.
Proverbs 17:9

Those who plan what is good find
love and faithfulness.
Proverbs 14:22

*i*f your marriage is coming in a distant second or third or fourth behind a lot of other "priorities," you need to grapple with reality. And reality says that if you don't start doing things differently, you have an excellent chance of becoming one more statistic, one more small part of the giant national average that says a marriage lasts some seven years and is gone.

In a word, you must prioritize within, and that means your spouse must come first. When your marriage comes first, everything else falls into its proper place.

For any couple—particularly the overly busy, hard-driving husbands and wives who are trying to juggle career and family—there is more reason than ever to seek refuge in each other, to have some times for yourselves. To keep your family together, you must start at the bottom—at the foundation of it all—your marriage relationship. Finding time for each other can be done—if you both really want to.

Dr. Kevin Leman
author of *What a Difference a Daddy Makes*

We must learn to trust and be trustworthy. Share your secret joys, your secret sorrows, your failings, your feelings of inadequacy, your fears and doubts, what makes you feel guilty. Do it in love and for love. Do it for your mate. Do it for yourself.

Is there something you've always wanted to share with your mate? Go ahead, take the risk. May the Holy Spirit mysteriously knit your hearts together in a deeper way than you ever imagined possible.

Patrick Morley

Communication skills are important to learn—no doubt about it—but they fall flat without love. They turn into tools of manipulation. "You're just doing that thing our counselor said to do" is the response a new technique often elicits in the absence of love. So before you try to tune up your talk, overhaul your heart. Allow love to seize every word, every syllable. Invite love to lay claim to your conversation.

Les and Leslie Parrott

Listen to Him

Listen to how he feels about his greatest pleasures in life.

Listen to how he feels about his most difficult weekly challenge.

Listen to his favorite jokes.

Listen to how he feels about his least attractive feature.

Listen to how he feels about television sports.

Listen to how he feels about his greatest weakness.

Listen to how he feels about his greatest hope for the future.

Listen to how he feels about his childhood.

Listen to how he feels about his greatest strength.

Listen to how he feels about his job.

*F*orgiveness is a key element in healthy long-term marriages. Forgiveness is the oil that lubricates a love relationship, and it's an oil we need daily. Forgiveness is not a one-time event; it's an attitude of wanting to partner with your spouse in spite of his or her imperfections and irritations.

Is there something right now that disappoints you about your mate or your relationship? Grievances can range in intensity from habitually leaving the TV on to having illicit affairs. No matter where your disappointments and hurts fall on the continuum, you must decide to forgive your spouse and move beyond these grievances before you can work on developing an exuberant, growing marriage.

Remember, forgiveness begins with a simple decision, a simple act of the will. We are to forgive as God has forgiven us. It is not dependent upon our spouse asking for our forgiveness or even acknowledging he or she has done anything wrong.

David and Claudia Arp

"I will love you when times are good or bad. I will cherish you even if I am upset with you. I will honor you at all times." Every couple can profit from saying these simple words to each other every day. The more each person can find new and creative ways to swear this commitment, the better. For instance, some part of it can be put into a lunch sack, engraved inside a bracelet, scribbled on a refrigerator note in the morning, contained in a love letter, or written in the sky above a football game.

The idea is to recite this vow over and over so that when the rocky times come, as they inevitably will, the commitment to love, honor, and cherish will trigger new ideas in the brain about how to hold the marriage together.

Dr. Neil Clark Warren

Marriages can never be perfect because people are not perfect. Being human, every bride and groom has faults as well as virtues. We are at times gloomy, cranky, selfish, or unreasonable. We are a mixture of generous, altruistic feelings combined with self-seeking aims, petty vanities, and ambitions. We unite love and courage with selfishness and fear. Marriage is an alloy of gold and tin. If we expect more than this, we are doomed to disappointment.

Les and Leslie Parrott

There is no right or wrong time to praise your wife. She'll love it when you're alone or when you're with the children and friends. Make sure you don't limit your praise to public or private times. If you only praise her in public, she might suspect you're showing off for your friends. If you only praise her in private, she may feel you're embarrassed about doing it.

Gary Smalley

May you rejoice in the wife of your
youth … may you ever be captivated by her love.
Proverbs 5:18–19

Let love and faithfulness never leave you;
bind them around your neck,
write them on the tablet of your heart.
Proverbs 3:3

Let us consider how we may spur one another
on toward love and good deeds.
Hebrews 10:24

Your love has given me great joy
and encouragement.
Philemon 7

Encourage Each Other

Make out two sets of New Year's resolutions. One for
yourself, one for your spouse. Then compare.

Pray for each other everyday.

Write your spouse a note. The key word is "Appreciate."

Encourage your spouse today in something he or she must do.

Write your spouse a brief love letter for the month. Include these
words: "thoughtful," "caring," and "best."

Do not criticize in front of others.

Stick by your spouse at a party and draw him
or her into the conversation.

Compliment each other.

Freely discuss your opinions of the headline news.

Give advice in a loving way when he/she asks for it.

*H*usbands place surprising importance on having their wives as recreational companions. The commercial caricature of men out in the wilderness, cold beer in hand, saying, "It doesn't get any better than this," is false. It can get a lot better than that when a wife joins her husband in a shared activity that he enjoys.

Don't allow you and your partner to drift apart because you can't find something enjoyable to do together. We have seen too many marriages fizzle because a wife didn't use her creative energies to build enjoyable moments of fun and relaxation with her husband. Make a careful list of recreational interests your husband enjoys. Next, circle those activities that you might find somewhat pleasurable. You can probably find a good half-dozen activities that you can enjoy with your husband. Your next task is to schedule these activities into your recreational time together.

If you learn to meet your husband's need for recreational companionship, you will discover that you are not only husband and wife, but best friends too.

Les and Leslie Parrott

O ver the last two decades, marriage specialists have researched the ingredients of a happy marriage. As a result, we know more about building a successful marriage today than ever before. For example, happily married couples will have:

Healthy expectations of marriage

A realistic concept of love

A positive attitude and outlook toward life

The ability to communicate their feelings

An understanding and acceptance of their gender differences

The ability to make decisions and settle arguments

A common spiritual foundation and goal

Every couple should be aware of these issues before (and after) they marry. Taking the time to understand these issues is like investing in an insurance policy against divorce.

Les and Leslie Parrott

A husband's responsibility can be summarized in one phrase: Love your wife! Your calling as a wife can also be summed up in a few words: Respond to your husband! You must remember there is only one way to convince your husband that you love him, and that is by your loving response—a response that he can see, hear, touch, feel, and enjoy on a daily basis, a response that includes the physical, but also touches every aspect of his life. This is your contribution to a love-filled, lasting marriage. Many wives who have enjoyed lifelong love affairs with their husbands say that this is their secret of success.

Ed Wheat

Talk Together

Talk about what each of you thinks is "romantic."

Agree upon two foods that will never be served at home.

Decide on one special thing each person
could do for his or her in-laws.

Negotiate who will shop for which relatives at Christmas.

Decide together approximately how much time you need to reserve
for just the two of you to be together in an average week.

Decide on a night each of you can go out with friends this week.

Negotiate what your next major purchase should be.

Suggest one book each person wants the other to read.

Negotiate times for each of you to exercise or play sports.

Discuss the amount of time it takes for both of you
to do the weekend chores. Divide the chores in such a way
that both of you agree is fair.

*E*xamine your typical schedules, and pick times when you can focus on each other's feelings, concerns, and interests. This could be at dinner, but it may work better just before going to sleep. Try lying in each other's arms and talking about how you feel—what is causing joy, what is causing anxiety and concern. Make it a time to be open and honest, but avoid attacking and complaining.

Dr. Kevin Leman
author of *What a Difference a Daddy Makes*

*W*hen forgiveness is truly necessary, forgive as quickly as you can, because forgiving has two good results: The first is your own release, and the second is the possibility of reconciliation between you and your mate.

Lewis Smedes

But the fruit of the Spirit is love, joy, peace,
patience, kindness, goodness, faithfulness,
gentleness and self-control.
Galatians 5:22

Dear friends, since God so loved us,
we also ought to love one another.
1 John 4:11

May the Lord make your love increase
and overflow for each other.
1 Thessalonians 3:12

Husbands ought to love their wives as their own
bodies. He who loves his wife loves himself.
Ephesians 5:28

*M*en have a tough time realizing that offering a listening ear is all a woman needs at times—or a comforting hug, a loving statement like "You are hurting, aren't you?" or "You are under a lot of pressure, aren't you?" Listening to your wife talk without offering quick solutions is the only way to meet her need to be known.

Les and Leslie Parrott

*P*riorities act as filters through which we can filter our day-to-day decisions because we have decided *in advance* what is most important.

A husband and wife will have other priorities, like work, rest, recreation, and ministry. However, loving God, loving each other, and loving our children form the indispensable core of a happy marriage. Notice the common denominator of love.

Patrick Morley

Tips for Loving Him

Give him a foot massage.

Surprise him with breakfast in bed.

Give him a Saturday off.

Buy a magazine he would enjoy reading.

Send him a fax.

Don't mention his hair loss—he already knows.

Buy yourself something sexy—for him.

Say you are sorry.

Write "I love you" on the steamy mirror
when he's in the shower.

Make him laugh.

Tips for Staying in Love

Concentrate on building an intimate relationship.

Nurture each other emotionally.

Touch lovingly, share thoughts and feelings.

Spend private time together so that you can continue
to feel secure and at home in each other's presence.

Avoid the negatives that could change the way you see
each other. Live in an atmosphere of approval,
and forgive quickly and generously.

Live out your commitment to one another
in such a way that strong links of trust
are established and maintained.

Build your marriage on a solid biblical base. Always
think and talk in "forever" terms.

Ed Wheat

Ask any couple who has been happily married for fifty years if their love life was a cakewalk. You'll be hard pressed to find one. Sure, many seasoned couples focus their memories on the positive side, but every lifelong couple who can look back over the decades together has endured tough times. You can be sure of that. And you can be sure of one other thing: They persevered, not because of legal or social constraints, but because love endures to the last.

Les and Leslie Parrott

Just for Fun

Go for a walk in the park. Take your camera
and get snapshots of each other.

Write your spouse a brief love letter. Spray your favorite
perfume on the paper to give it a special touch.

Go to an amusement park.

Pack a little basket of your favorite snacks and watch fireworks.

Go to a nearby park and play on the swings.

Play miniature golf without competing.

Go to the zoo and imitate the animals.

Start laughing and see who can laugh the longest.

Take bread to a nearby pond and feed the fish.

Find a good taffy recipe and make it together.
Have fun pulling the taffy!

*P*hysical contact is a powerful means of communicating and a gentle and supportive way to nourish the spirit and convey positive emotions. Imagine for a moment that you come home from a tough day, feeling tense, tired, and irritable—but then your partner wraps you in his or her arms and gives you a loving squeeze. That hug causes a rise in hemoglobin, a substance in the red blood cells that transports energizing oxygen throughout your body. Incredibly, that gentle hug or even a soft caress can cause a speeding heart to quiet, soaring blood pressure to drop, and severe pain to ease.

Given its potent impact on our lives, it's no wonder that touch is known as the "mother of the senses." There is simply no better way to communicate the idea that "you are not alone," or "I love you." So the next time you're at a loss for words, remember, touching may be the best way of speaking to your partner.

Les and Leslie Parrott

Criticism may seem fairly harmless, even "constructive" under certain circumstances. Yet it has the potential to bring about the slow, painful death of a love relationship: when criticism drips unchecked, love dies by inches. The deadly destroyer of marriage, criticism should be replaced by encouragement and edification.

Ed Wheat

Commitment creates a small island of certainty in the swirling waters of uncertainty. As the mooring of marriage, commitment secures love for our partner when passion burns low and when turbulent times and fierce impulses overtake us.

Les and Leslie Parrott

Listen to Her

Listen to how she feels about the amount
of time you spend with her.

Listen to how she feels about in-laws.

Listen as she recalls her best Christmas memory.

Listen to how she feels about your sex life.

Listen to how she feels about her parents.

Listen to how she feels about the amount of time
the two of you actually spend talking to each other.

Listen to how she feels about the amount
of time you spend talking with the children.

Listen to how she feels about the family budget.

Listen to how she feels about working
or not working outside of the home.

Listen to how she feels about planning fun times.

Serve one another in love.
Galatians 5:13

Knowledge puffs up, but love builds up.
1 Corinthians 8:1

Many waters cannot quench love;
rivers cannot wash it away.
Song of Songs 8:7

He who pursues righteousness and love
finds life, prosperity and honor.
Proverbs 21:21

Praying for your mate is another way of saying, "I love you." It is an expression of loyalty to our partner…. Pray for your spouse every day. You may be the only person in the entire world willing to pray for your mate on a regular basis. Occasionally affirm your husband or wife by letting him or her know you are praying. Ask how he or she would like you to pray specifically. Finally be faithful over the long haul. Imagine the surprise when your partner finds out the wonderful thing that has happened as an answer to your prayers.

Patrick Morley

A woman loves to find hidden notes—in her jewelry box, the silver drawer, the medicine cabinet. Search for ways to praise your wife. The possibilities are endless.

Gary Smalley

*W*ithin a marriage, an apology to your partner that is sincerely meant is much more than a civility—it can be a powerful tool for resolving issues and strengthening your relationship.

True apologies in marriage can happen only when partners come to understand accountability. This is another way of saying that each of you must take responsibility for your own behavior, acknowledge your partner's point of view, and at times own up to things about yourself you don't like. Finally, it may mean making changes.

All couples need a healing mechanism, a way to run a new page in marriage, and knowing how and when to say you're sorry can make a big difference. An apology may not be a literal "I'm sorry"; it may be giving gifts, sharing an evening out, or simply taking a quiet walk together. The point is that a sincere apology, whatever its form, leaves the couple with a renewed closeness and a relieved feeling that all is well.

Les and Leslie Parrott

*H*ere are a few nonverbal ways to show
your husband how important he is:

Be attentive to his concerns when he comes home.
Look as attractive as possible when he comes home.
Prepare appetizing meals.
Show interest and ask questions about his job,
activities, problems, achievements.
Listen attentively by focusing your eyes on him.
Don't make him compete with the TV, the dishes,
or even the children when he's trying to talk to you.

Gary Smalley

*L*oving couples use every opportunity to boost each other in front
of other people and to cast each other in the best light—much as
they did in their courting days, when they wanted their friends
and family to like their new love. They say things like, "Sarah just
got a promotion, but she won't tell you that." Or, "Rick may not
mention it, but he secured a huge grant for his company this
week." Loving couples praise one another in private and in public.
They tell each other's stories of accomplishment.

Les and Leslie Parrott

Add some adventure to your love life. Try a little spontaneity. If you always make love in the evening, try mornings. Call in late for work and grab a couple of hours with each other while you are fresh. Plan a middle-of-the-day rendezvous. One couple, who both work downtown, took a picnic basket to work and met at a downtown motel on their lunch break. Another couple, on a more austere budget, met during their afternoon break in their car in the parking garage for hugs and kisses. Go on and brainstorm. You're only limited by your imagination! Try some variety in when and where you make love. Remember, variety can be the spice of life. Be explorers.

David and Claudia Arp

Just Do it

Begin each day with a hug and a kiss.

Don't miss a birthday or special day.
Write them on a calendar.

Decorate Christmas cookies together.

Hang her picture in your office.

Share a hug and a kiss at midnight on New Year's Eve.

Convince him to do something silly —just with you.

Write your spouse a note using "Thoughtful" as a key word.

Make a taco salad together for dinner.

Go through all your clothes and give away any clothes
you do not wear anymore.

Both of you put the kids to bed this evening. Be creative and
tell a bedtime story that the two of you have made up together.

Brag about your spouse to other people behind his/her back.

When you initiate sex from time to time, use imagination to make the bedroom and your appearance as inviting as possible. Perfume, candlelight, gentle words, and a soft touch are just a few of the ways you can add creativity to the occasion.

Another way to make the occasion more fulfilling for you and your husband is for each of you to concentrate on meeting each other's sexual needs. I have found that a selfless, giving attitude contributes most to sexual enjoyment. A man's greatest fulfillment comes when he puts his whole heart into stimulating his wife and bringing her to a climactic experience. At the same time, a woman is most fulfilled when she concentrates on meeting her husband's needs. Selfish sex does nothing but remove the potential for maximum pleasure. Sex at its best happens when a husband begins to meet his wife's emotional needs on a daily basis. All the techniques and atmosphere in the world can't warm up a neglected wife.

Gary Smalley

*C*ommunication squeezed in during half-time activities or the commercial breaks will be unsatisfying and, even worse, is the effort to talk something over while the television continues to blare and one partner tries to keep an eye on a favorite program. So forego television, put away the video movies, turn off the radio, and shut down the stereo. Close the doors, get your children (if any) occupied elsewhere, and take the telephone off the hook. Never listen with split attention. The communication system of your marriage deserves the very best.

Ed Wheat

Enjoy Each Other

Make a list of things you do together that bring you joy.
Set dates to do these things together.

Do some form of exercise together today.

Go to a card shop and find romantic cards for each other.
Buy your favorite one and give it with a special note inside.

Put away the laundry together.

Reminisce about the day you met.
Try to duplicate the conversation from your first date.

Have a "just for two" candlelight dinner.

Work together on the lawn or garden.

Go to a Chinese restaurant and try
something you have never eaten before.

Sing songs you liked when you were dating.

*H*ere are a few tips for cultivating politeness in your marriage:

Greet each other with an acknowledgment and warm hello, and mark a leaving with a tender good-bye.
When your partner has done a chore, always show appreciation for the job even if the way it was done doesn't meet with your approval (say "Thanks for washing the car" rather than "You missed a spot").
Surround meal times with pleasant conversations. Shut off the TV and pay attention to your mate instead.

Research has shown that it takes only one put-down to undo hours of kindness that you give to your partner. So the most gracious offering of politeness you can give your partner is to avoid putdowns altogether.

Les and Leslie Parrott

Better a meal of vegetables where there is love
than a fattened calf with hatred.
Proverbs 15:17

Love covers over all wrongs.
Proverbs 10:12

Place me like a seal over your heart,
like a seal on your arm;
for love is as strong as death,
its jealousy unyielding as the grave.
It burns like blazing fire,
like a mighty flame.
Song of Songs 8:6

If you have any encouragement from being united with
Christ, if any comfort from his love … then make my joy
complete by being like-minded, having the same love,
being one in spirit and purpose.
Philippians 2:1–2

*W*hat has happened to all the loveable characteristics that first attracted your husband to you? Perhaps it was your quiet, gentle voice … your gentle spirit … your ability to listen … your vivacious personality … your keen mind … your sense of humor … whatever qualities made the total person to whom he was initially attracted. Have some of them gotten lost through the years? Do you scream for his attention now? Are you too busy to listen to him? Have you lost your sense of humor? If you are to recapture his attention, you must somehow recapture and exhibit those qualities unique to you that first drew him to you.

Gary Smalley

To be autonomous is a universal male need. Whenever a man is under stress (an important deadline is approaching, he is under pressure at work, etc.), he requires a little space. At such times he becomes absentminded, unresponsive, absorbed, and preoccupied. Unlike women, men typically don't want to talk about the situation, they don't want to be held or comforted—not until they have had time to themselves.

Part of the need for autonomy is the man's need to have time to regroup. Some wives complain because their husbands don't immediately talk about their day when they come home from work. They first want to read the paper or water the lawn, anything to clean their mind before engaging in the relationship. It's a male thing. But giving your husband space when he needs it, whether you understand it or not, will gain you a happier husband.

Les and Leslie Parrott

*L*ove must be learned, and learned again and again; there is no end to it.

Katherine Anne Porter

*i*nsensitivity is like trampling with clodhopper boots over the other person—not out of malice, but ignorance. Love pays the most careful attention to the beloved. Anyone can learn to be sensitive to another person.

Ed Wheat

*R*emember, it's the little things that really matter. Little things like coming home early and taking her out to dinner at a place she really likes (not the Colonel). Like sending her a note home from the office—handwritten—that says, "I want you to know how much I care. I want you to know how much I appreciate all you do for our family. You do so much for me and for the children. I'm so proud of you."

Dr. Kevin Leman
author of *What a Difference a Daddy Makes*

Tips for Loving Her

Surprise her with a card or flowers.

Express how much you appreciate her.

Pray for her to enjoy God's best in life.

Let her take a bubble bath while you do the dishes.

Help her finish her goals—hobbies or education.

Get rid of habits that annoy her.

Do not expect a band to play whenever you help
with the housecleaning.

Tell her you love her—often.

Give her an engraved plaque assuring
her of your lasting love.

Practice common courtesies like holding
the door for her or pouring her coffee.

Kindness comes from small behaviors. We don't think of big donations or grand contributions as "kind." We call them "generous," "charitable," or "benevolent," but it is the small things we call "kind." Kindness, for example, comes when we turn down our partner's side of the bed before crawling into it ourselves. Kindness comes when we readjust the car seat after driving so our partner doesn't have to. Kindness comes when we load the dishwasher when it's not our turn. Kindness comes from a million small behaviors that enhance the life of the one we love.

Les and Leslie Parrott

This is my prayer: that your love may abound more and more in knowledge and depth of insight.
Philippians 1:9

However, each one of you also must love his wife as he loves himself, and the wife must respect her husband.
Ephesians 5:33

The only thing that counts is faith expressing itself through love.
Galatians 5:6

Sow for yourselves righteousness, reap the fruit of unfailing love.
Hosea 10:12

Two of the most important lovemaking skills and romance enhancers are listening with your heart and talking to your spouse while you are loving each other. Your love life may be active, but if it is all action and no talk, you're missing an added dimension of romance. Tell your mate what you like. Use a little body language. Nobody is a mind reader!

If you find it difficult to talk about the intimate side of your relationship, start by reading a book together. You may find that this is less threatening, and it may open the door for conversation—and who knows what doors conversation may open!

David and Claudia Arp

One of the best ways to keep the imagination alive in your relationship is to be well-informed. Ask your friends how they add creativity to their marriages. Read books and magazines about subjects that would stimulate interesting conversation. My wife contributes so much to the variety of our marriage because she is constantly learning. She not only keeps her mind alert by reading, but she also takes courses on nutrition, gourmet cooking, and other special subjects. It seems she always has something new and interesting to talk about.

Gary Smalley

Don't forget that one of a husband's basic needs is admiration and respect. You'll never know how many points you can put in his Love Bank by slipping a note into his lunch or jacket pocket that says, "You're such a wonderful husband and such a great dad. The kids and I are so lucky that you belong to us."

Dr. Kevin Leman
author of *What a Difference a Daddy Makes*

Ideas for Dating

Reminisce about the things during this past year
that have drawn you closer together.

Address Christmas cards together and reminisce about
the good times spent with those family members and friends.

Go to a bookstore and pick out a book for each other.

Attend a high school or college sporting event.

Try a Mexican restaurant for dinner.

Find a comfortable spot outside to lay back and watch the stars.

Make plans for a weekend trip.

Go to a French restaurant for dinner.

Bake and decorate a cake together.

Read poetry to each other.

*L*oving couples negotiate. They talk through something to find a mutually satisfying compromise. It's not that hard, really. You probably did it without thinking when you were dating and oh-so-willing to consider the other person's wishes.

Winston Churchill once said, "The English never draw a line without blurring it." That should be true of the couple who learns to compromise. When a husband and wife come to believe that equality means splitting things precisely down the middle, then marriage becomes a contest of who can get a better deal. And that wipes out the true spirit of compromise. Finding an agreeable solution to disagreements means that sometimes one or the other partner gets a bigger piece of the pie.

Les and Leslie Parrott

*I*f you develop a positive attitude, not only will others want to be around you more often, but your wife will also benefit tremendously. She will have a greater sense of worth and value, knowing you have provided the encouragement only a husband can give.

Encourage your wife and deepen your marriage relationship by learning how to praise her. Promise yourself to tell your wife daily what you appreciate about her. Promise yourself—not her—because she might develop expectations and be hurt if you forget. Begin by learning to verbalize your thoughts of appreciation.

Gary Smalley

*E*very husband and every wife is different and has different ways of giving and receiving love. For some people touch is the primary language of love. Their spouse can say, "I love you" twenty times a day but without an embrace or a kiss or a squeeze they won't feel loved. Other people need to hear verbal expressions of love. They need to hear in concrete terms why their spouse loves them. Service is what makes some people feel most loved. They respond best to affection that is revealed in practical terms. Gifts make other people feel loved—not because of the cost involved, but because of the personal attention and thought that goes into them. Spending time together makes other people feel loved. They don't care particularly what they and their spouses do, as long as they are together.

Bill and Lynne Hybels

How beautiful you are and how pleasing,
O love, with your delights!
Song of Songs 7:6

Do everything in love.
1 Corinthians 16:14

I pray that you, being rooted and established in
love, may have power … to grasp how wide and
long and high and deep is the love of Christ.
Ephesians 3:17–18

Be encouraged in heart and united in love.
Colossians 2:2

*W*omen need praise. We should be able to understand their need because we, too, want to know that we are of value to other people. One of the ways we know we're needed is when others express appreciation for who we are and what we do. When you praise your wife, it's important to use words and actions that communicate praise from her point of view. Anything that is romantic or deals with building deeper relationships usually pleases wives.

Gary Smalley

Tips for Loving Him

Tell him how attractive he is.

Wash and powder or lotion his feet tonight.

Pray for him.

Write him a love letter for Valentine's Day.

Wash and vacuum his car.

Let him have "the guys" over.

Laugh with him, not at him.

Just be yourself.

Listen.

Tell him what is wrong.

Tips for Loving Her

Let her sleep late on Saturday morning.

Massage her neck and shoulders.

Bring home a music tape you think she will enjoy.

Buy her a magazine she will enjoy reading.

Offer to take the kids out on Saturday.

Change the oil in her car.

Water her plants.

Put the toilet seat down.

Make a date for lunch.

Be nice to her mother.

Talk Together

Negotiate some quiet time for each of you when the other spouse is in charge of the children.

Decide on a budget for leisure time and vacation activities.

Share something interesting that you read this week.

Share with each other what your needs are in making love.

Discuss your hopes and dreams for the future.

Share what your favorite television show is and watch both of them together.

Evaluate your bedtime hour.

Talk about how you have felt when former boyfriends or girlfriends have been brought up in conversations. Decide if you want to agree not to mention these people again.

Discuss how you feel about your spiritual growth as a couple.

Talk about people you would like to have over for a meal. Choose one person or family and invite them over in the coming week.

As God's chosen people, holy and dearly loved,
clothe yourselves with compassion, kindness,
humility, gentleness and patience.
Colossians 3:12

Where you go I will go, and where you
stay I will stay. Your people will be my
people and your God my God.
Ruth 1:16

How delightful is your love,
my sister, my bride!
How much more pleasing is
your love than wine,
and the fragrance of your
perfume than any spice!
Song of Songs 4:10

Love each other.
John 15:17

*E*mpathy is perhaps the toughest work of building a strong marriage. Because most of us are wired to use either our head or heart, one more than the other, it takes a conscious effort to empathize. Empathy, however, brings together both sympathetic and analytic abilities, both heart and head, to fully understand our partners. Empathy says, "If I were you, I would act as you do; I understand why you feel the way you feel."

Empathy always involves risk, so be forewarned. Accurately understanding your partner's hurts and hopes will change you—but the benefits of taking that risk far outweigh the disadvantages. Once you consciously feel his or her feelings and understand his or her perspective, you will see the world differently.

Les and Leslie Parrott

*R*omance depends on your attitude and perspective. Too often we take ourselves and our mates too seriously. Or we always hurry. Remember, whatever you do to promote romance, getting there is half the fun. Making time for love will help you be good to each other. Take time to unwind from your busy day; make the transition slowly. Go for a walk and hold hands. Stop along the way for a kiss or two. Taking time to kiss and cuddle and laugh and share intimate thoughts during your lovemaking will add romance.

David and Claudia Arp

When a husband and wife come together after an absence—upon waking, getting home from work, or returning from a trip—the first few minutes will set the stage for how the rest of the time will go. Family therapist Marcia Lasswell says, "It's very important that the first few minutes of reconnection be positive and supportive. We all know how good it feels to walk into someone's presence and have them look up and smile, and how awful it is if he or she is preoccupied or negative." We know this because the "it's-good-to-see-you" look is what we instinctively gave, and received, in the early stages of our dating relationship.

Les and Leslie Parrott

Tips for Loving Him

Write him a note. The key word is "Adore."

Pretend you think his old car is awesome.

Buy him his favorite candy.

Warm up the car for him on cold mornings.

Leave a message on his answering machine.

Leave notes in different pockets of his jeans.

Run an errand he hates to do.

Take him out for dinner.

Laugh at the jokes you've heard 10 times.

Believe in him.

Don't mention his weight gain,
he already knows about it.

You probably weren't somber and sad when your husband married you. So, if you want to be his best friend now, you may need to add a little humor to your relationship. No need to buy a clown suit. Just look for ways to tickle his funny bone. Clip those comics or cartoons that strike you as funny and save them for his enjoyment during lighthearted times. Be willing to loosen up and laugh heartily when he tells a good joke. There are countless ways to add humor to your marriage. Be willing to set aside the serious quest for romance at times to enjoy just having fun together as friends.

Gary Smalley

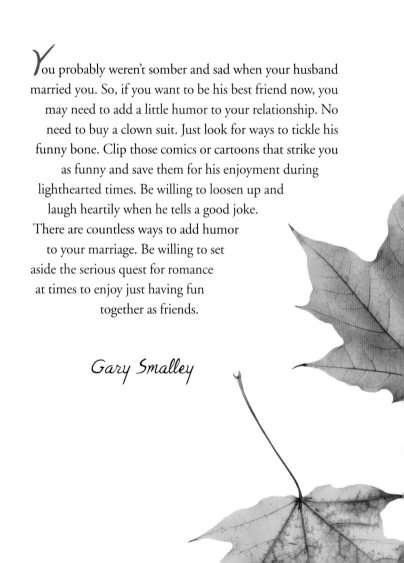

*E*very successful marriage is the result of two people working diligently and skillfully to cultivate their love. When they combine passion, intimacy, and commitment, they are able to grow a flourishing, healthy marriage.

Les and Leslie Parrott

A comfortable, orderly home which offers a peaceful atmosphere makes for marital happiness. Creative clutter is one thing; messiness which drives your partner (and you, too) "up the wall" needs to be remedied. God, truly, is the God of order, not of confusion. Many fine "help" books are available to take you through this problem. When one determines to keep a perfect house, that also can cause discomfort and unhappiness. Your goal should be a home you both can enjoy and the freedom to invite people into your house without worrying about its "disaster area" appearance.

Ed Wheat

Love is patient, love is kind.
It does not envy,
it does not boast,
it is not proud. It is not rude,
it is not self-seeking, it is not
easily angered, it keeps no record
of wrongs. Love does not delight
in evil but rejoices with the truth.
It always protects, always trusts,
always hopes, always
perseveres. Love never fails.
1 Corinthians 13:4–8

Live a life of love, just as
Christ loved us.
Ephesians 5:2

Ideas for Dating

Visit a pet shop and look for the most exotic pet.

Decorate your home with lights at Christmas.

Take an early spring bike ride.

Go to the movies and see a comedy. Laugh!

Look over new homes for features you both like.

Go to the florist and pick out a plant.

Take a drive, and flip a penny at each crossroad to
determine which way to turn.

Go fishing together.

Take an early morning walk
and enjoy the outdoors together.

Play a board game together.

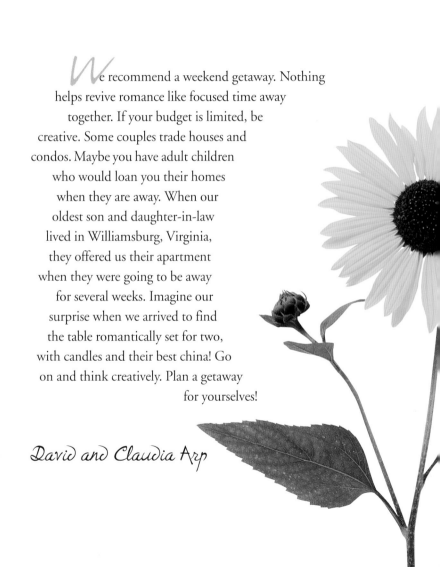

We recommend a weekend getaway. Nothing helps revive romance like focused time away together. If your budget is limited, be creative. Some couples trade houses and condos. Maybe you have adult children who would loan you their homes when they are away. When our oldest son and daughter-in-law lived in Williamsburg, Virginia, they offered us their apartment when they were going to be away for several weeks. Imagine our surprise when we arrived to find the table romantically set for two, with candles and their best china! Go on and think creatively. Plan a getaway for yourselves!

David and Claudia Arp

Tips for Loving Her

Help her think beyond tomorrow.
Let her sleep late.
Plant a rose bush for her.
Scrub the floor.
Calm her fears.
Rub her feet.
Let her go out with her friends.
Brush the snow off her car.
Let her cry.
Clear a path to her car on a snowy morning.

*I*f you want to reclaim table time with your spouse, make it a pleasant time that both of you look forward to. You don't have to cook like Julia Child or set a table like Martha Stewart to make mealtimes pleasurable. What matters most is the focus of your conversation. Don't allow it to be a time of dumping your problems on your partner. When your spouse asks you how your day was, even if it was horrendous, say, "I'll tell you in a minute, but right now it's good to be home with you." Set the tone for an evening that will be uplifting, spontaneous, and positive. Give your partner your attention before you give him or her your problems.

Les and Leslie Parrott

*H*ave you ever thought of applying all you know about good manners and courtesy in your times of relating sexually? The purpose of etiquette is to smooth and improve human relations. Many sexual problems result from ignoring bedroom etiquette, and good manners in the sexual relationship could cure some of the dysfunctions we must treat.

The truly courteous are warm, kind, generous, and flexible in the bedroom. They consider one another's needs and feelings, and approach sex with their partner not as a right, but a privilege. Courtesy is made up of tact and foresight—looking ahead to see how what you say or do will affect another person. Tact means to touch delicately. As a considerate lover, you will try to relate to your loved one with this "delicacy of touch," and you will avoid being careless or rude in the name of relaxed intimacy.

Ed Wheat

Tips for Staying Romantic

Try incorporating the following ingredients
into your personal romantic style.

The element of the unexpected. Anything that
is repeated month after month, year after year,
can easily become humdrum.

The element of dating. Laugh and
enjoy each other and be a little crazy.

The element of the impractical. Impractical
romantic events create moments to remember.

The element of creativity. Discover what delights your
partner and then make those delights happen in creative ways.

The element of the daily. Romance involves
daily acts of care, concern, love, listening and giving
each other your personal attention.

The element of commitment. If commitment to each
other is at the heart of your marriage, romance will thrive.

H. Norman Wright

We hope you will find time to pace yourself, to stoke your own fire, and make your love relationship a priority. Take it from our friends Dave and Jeanne: it can just keep getting better and better as the years go by. "Romance doesn't have to die out," said Dave. "It can grow and blossom through all your married years, if you continue to show your love in physical ways plus loving words and deeds. God designed man and woman to enjoy each other in marriage, and we find that enjoyment still growing after forty-five years of marriage."

Let us encourage you to fan the fires of romance. You never know where it might lead. Go on and take the risk. Stoke your own fire and enjoy your marriage with your lover and your best friend.

David and
Claudia Arp

Enjoy Each Other

Remember what you first loved about each other.

Cuddle up and relive your first date.
What would you want to be the same?
What would you want to be different?

Go out and purchase the largest pumpkin you
can find. Carve out the pumpkin and bake the
pumpkin seeds for a snack later.

Visit a hobby shop and look for something you
would enjoy doing together.

Stroll through the mall holding hands.

Get dressed up and go to a fancy restaurant with friends.

Check the newspaper to find a play or concert to attend.

Take an early morning walk and look
for signs of the season changing.

Lay in front of the fire together and dream about the future.

The ideal day of romance, according to survey results, included breakfast in bed, a picnic in the country, or an elegant dinner. Jacuzzis figured prominently in the response. So did the element of surprise and the absence of interruptions. One woman said her ideal day of romance was simple: "He'd never call his office or take calls on his portable phone."

The message is clear, men. We don't have to be a Mel Gibson or a Brad Pitt to make love exciting. We don't have to spend money like Donald Trump to be romantic. Women admire enduring love over all-consuming passion, time and again. They aren't looking for expensive preprogrammed evenings. They'll take the spontaneous heartfelt gesture of love every time.

Les and Leslie Parrott

Tips for Loving Her

Pretend you like her cat.

Put her favorite candy bar in her purse.

Hold hands in public.

Take out the garbage without being asked.

Share her dreams.

Give her time to herself.

Tell her she's not getting older, just better.

Notice what she is wearing and compliment her.

Tell her you are glad you married her.

Ideas for Dating

Pack a basket with a healthy dinner
and go to a park for a picnic.

Assemble and wrap your Christmas packages together.

Go to the lake shore and walk barefoot in the sand.

Organize your vacation pictures and
write captions for them.

Share an early morning breakfast on a
Saturday morning at a local restaurant to
make the weekend seem longer.

Over coffee at your favorite bookstore,
discuss the best book you have ever read.

Rent a sports car for the weekend
and go for a long ride.

Play Scrabble together.

Watch the sunset from your front porch or from a hilltop.

Go to a driving range and hit a bucket of golf balls.

Sources

100 Ways to Say I Love You. Grand Rapids, MI: ZondervanPublishingHouse, 1993.

Arp, David and Claudia. *The Second Half of Marriage.* © 1996 by David and Claudia Arp. Grand Rapids, MI: ZondervanPublishingHouse, 1996.

Couple's Devotional Bible. Grand Rapids, MI: ZondervanPublishingHouse, 1994.

Crabb, Larry, et al. *Bring Home the Joy.* Grand Rapids, MI: ZondervanPublishingHouse, 1998.

Hybels, Bill and Lynne. *Fit to Be Tied.* © 1991 by Bill and Lynne Hybels. Grand Rapids, MI: ZondervanPublishingHouse, 1993.

Leman, Dr. Kevin. *Keeping Your Family Together When the World is Falling Apart,* Used by permission of the author.

Morley, Patrick. *Devotions for Couples.* ©1994 by Patrick Morley. Grand Rapids, MI: ZondervanPublishing House, 1994.

Parrott, Drs. Les and Leslie. *Like a Kiss on the Lips.* © 1997 by Les and Leslie Parrott. Grand Rapids, MI: ZondervanPublishingHouse, 1997. *Love is …* © 1999 by Les and Leslie Parrott. Grand Rapids, MI: ZondervanPublishingHouse, 1999. *Saving Your Marriage Before It Starts.* © 1995 by Les and Leslie Parrott. Grand Rapids, MI: ZondervanPublishingHouse, 1995.

Richards, Larry and Sue. *Keeping Your Love Alive.* Grand Rapids, MI: ZondervanPublishingHouse, 1996.

Smalley, Gary. *For Better or for Best.* © 1982 by The Zondervan Corporation. Grand Rapids, MI: ZondervanPublishingHouse, 1982. *The Hidden Keys of a Loving, Lasting Marriage* © 1984, 1988 by Gary Smalley. Grand Rapids, MI: ZondervanPublishingHouse, 1988. *The Joy of Committed Love.* © 1984 by Gary Smalley. Grand Rapids, MI: ZondervanPublishingHouse, 1984.

Warren, Ph.D., Neil Clark. *Learning to Live with the Love of Your Life and Loving It!* (formerly published under the title *The Triumphant Marriage*) a Focus on the Family book published by Tyndale House. Copyright © 1995 by Neil Clark Warren, Ph.D.

Wheat, Ed. *The First Years of Forever.* Grand Rapids, MI: ZondervanPublishingHouse, 1988.

keeping your

love

keeping your

love alive

love

love

love alive

keeping your

love

keeping your